MIDNIGHT STREAMS

Canticum Caritatis
(A Song of Charity)

by Michael J. Hoogasian

We can all try but inevitably fall short of describing God's Great Love. Here is my current attempt. As I continue to give thanks and praise to and through the Lord Jesus Christ, may the following words glorify the Heavenly Father through Christ in the unity of the Holy Spirit. And so, to that glory, I dedicate this to all those who have been moved by the wonder of God's presence to do great things for His Kingdom.

In accord with canon 829 of the Code of Canon Law, I hereby grant approval to publish Midnight Streams Canticum Caritatis by Michael J. Hoogasian.

Most Reverend Robert J. McManus, S.T.D.
Bishop of Worcester
Diocese of Worcester
August 25, 2015

The Imprimatur ("Permission to Publish") is a declaration that a book is considered to be free from doctrinal or moral error. It is not implied that those who have granted the Imprimatur agree with the contents, opinions, or statements expressed.

Printed by Lulu.com 2013, 2015

ISBN: 978-1-300-65738-5

Illustrations created from modified public domain clipart.

A Sharkangel Book

SHARKANGEL

The SHARKANGEL symbol combines the author's reverent connection to St. Michael the Archangel, guardian of Christ's faithful, and his childlike fascination with great white sharks.

"By day may the LORD send his mercy, and by night may his righteousness be with me! I will pray to the God of my life…" (Psalms 42:9 NAB)

Regarding Midnight Streams

No doubt, we have all been up late at night, past a normal bedtime hour when deep thoughts and ideas are running rampant. During these restless times, our speech tends to flow freely in both familiar and strange company. We become vulnerable to sharing secrets, perceptions, and experiences that under different, more natural circumstances would be locked away in our mind's vault. Honesty seems so easy, while trust and confidence a guarantee. Alone, it is within these moments, during these so called "ungodly" hours, where many life-altering decisions and events may occur. Inspiration stimulates its greatest visions, provoking the genius within to have such amazing feelings of insight and creativity.

"Midnight Streams" is a phrase I use to capture the essence of the cognitive events that transpire during such occasions. Thoughts, though often sporadic, flow in *streams* of consciousness concerning all aspects of life. Frequently influenced by a particular day's occurrences, ideas regarding daily and life-long choices, social interactions, senses of duty and purpose, the search for meaning in an otherwise meaningless existence all generate an uneasy mind not settled yet for sleep. Amidst such confusion, organization is necessary to quiet many unanswerable questions and give peace to a weary head. Moreover, it is at these times, I feel, prayer is most useful and effective when applied with contemplation and patience. Writing becomes a highly beneficial tool in these situations, providing sense to sometimes overwhelming conceptions…

*   *   *

"See what love the Father has bestowed on us that we may be called the children of God. Yet so we are. The reason the world does not know us is that it did not know him. Beloved, we are God's children now; what we shall be has not yet been revealed. We do know that when it is revealed we shall be like him, for we shall see him as he is. Everyone who has this hope based on him makes himself pure, as he is pure." (1 John 1:1-3 NAB)

Love is an incredibly versatile word and its unfettered use causes people to misperceive a greater truth surrounding it. The many synonyms associated with it cause perception to change from small pleasures to deep emotional family connections. For instance, I *love* eating cookies with milk or when I put on a new pair of socks. I also *love* my parents and the rest of my family for all the guidance and support they've given me throughout my life. Clearly, these are not the same thing. So, depending on its context in common usage, "love" can be a trivial or great concern.

As far back as I can remember, I have been a contemplative person, incessantly searching for deeper wisdom on many aspects of the human experience. Love naturally became a primary focus of thought. In its purest form, as I trust now, love is a self-sacrificing term more synonymous with charity and compassion than feelings of self-gratification or a pleasurable emotion. I believe the word is best used in its most appropriate context by describing the ultimate spiritual relationship that eternally exists between the members of the Blessed

Trinity: Father, Son, and Holy Ghost. It is that same perfect love that God reveals to His creation through sacred scripture, the Church, nature, people of good will, and most completely through the life, ministry, death, and resurrection of Jesus Christ.

* * *

"He made from one the whole human race to dwell on the entire surface of the earth, and he fixed the ordered seasons and the boundaries of their regions, so that people might seek God, even perhaps grope for him and find him, though indeed he is not far from any one of us. (Acts 17:26-27 NAB)

Many of us, either by a determined will, fate or maybe chance, find ourselves pursuing various dreams in this game of life. It seems to me that the goal for all mankind should be to discover, yield to, develop, strengthen, and share this love which flows from God. In doing so, I am confident that individuals will find their true purposes and live a very blessed life regardless of worldly circumstance or perception.

* * *

"Teacher, which commandment in the law is the greatest?' He said to him, 'You shall love the Lord, your God, with all your heart, with all your soul, and with all your mind." (Matthew 22:36-37 NAB)

The following streams are the result of my contemplation of God's revelation of love to all mankind through His Holy Bible. As you read of all the love He has demonstrated since the beginning of time, it should stir within you a desire to fulfill this greatest of commandments: to love Him with all that we have. Created in His image, it is our true nature to love God in return with all that we are. Whether by the gift of life and creation itself, his admonishment of the chosen people from ancient history through the present, or demonstrated in the emptying of Himself in Christ, be humbled and accept into your heart the grace of God's omnipresent love. Let it move you to seek it more deeply for the glory of His Holy Name. And as always, I pray for you, my reader, in the name of the Father, the Son, and the Holy Spirit. Amen.

Enjoy…

Midnight Streams

Underneath a bright moonbeam

Minds swept away by a midnight stream.

Such calm waters under the sun

Storm after the day is done.

Flowing by all that you want,

Regretful choices torment and taunt.

Foggy memories along the shore

Enshroud lost loves you once adored.

Tossed and turned from side to side

Unleashed in your mind, no place to hide.

As rapids rage, then begin to dive

Within the mists continue to strive

And beneath cascades of midnight streams

Find, at last, your lifelong dreams.

Contents

I
The Beginning

The dark and empty eternal abyss:

The ideal place to fill with bliss.

With canvas blank, and paint endless

The piece is set for the Great Artist.[1]

With a word of power, lifting not Their hands,

They spoke into being the skies and the lands.

Lights were cast in spirals and bands,

Afar, white sparks like grains of sands.[2]

A nightly reminder in plain sight;
The heavens glow with arrays of light
With glory on high declaring right
A ceaseless song of God's great might.[3]

Then waters pooling under the dome
Where fish would soon call their home
Oceans raged with waves and foam
And rains would fall to fertile loam.[4]

And when complete with a smile and nod
They said, "This is good[5] because I AM[6] God."
And who could have made a cosmos quite like this?
The Father, Son, and Holy Ghost with canticum caritatis.

II
Garden Growth

Now the Godhead pleased, having readied the ground,
Filled it with seed for all plants to abound
With grace from the Word, a most Holy sound[7],
Every producer on Earth could soon be found.

Rich soil did respond to the Makers' every plea
Bringing forth short green shrubs and every tall fruit tree,
Herbs emerged and grasses appeared quite abundantly
While vegetables did flourish rather prolifically.

Ivy vines and leafy ferns sprouted in due time,
And brightly colored flowers blossomed down the line,
Near the mighty oaks and the all-majestic pines,
Each one a hearty gift bearing the Lovers' living signs.[8]

A third day was done; good work indeed pays,
For the moon and the sun were shining forth their rays.
Soothing lunar light followed bright solar blaze,[9]
The cosmic dancers would tango until the end of days.[10]

And when complete with a smile and nod
They said, "This is good because I AM God."
And who could have grown a garden quite like this?[11]
The Father, Son, and Holy Ghost with canticum caritatis.

III
The Living Planet

Seas then filled with various fish with shiny silver scale,
Swimming sharks, playful seals, and every kind of whale.
To make us awe and wonder as to what's beneath the veil,
Monsters like Leviathan do haunt the ancients' tales.[12]

Waters teemed deep below, yet above, the sky would bring,
Soaring birds, who sailed on soft feathered wing,
Whose graceful gift would often be to fly and sweetly sing
Memorial tunes of glory for the Great Creation King.[13]

Cattle, tigers, giraffes, the deer, and every beast on four
Walked across the plains and fields and even on the shore,
While insects and other creeping things hid on the forest floor,
Apes and squirrels played in the trees, and all created more![14]

'Twas according to the sanction that came from the Most High
Fruitful by assignment, it was instinct to comply
For They blessed the creatures telling them: "be fertile and multiply."
So the planet did fill quickly from the depths up to the sky![15]

And when complete with a smile and nod
They said, "This is good because I AM God."
And who could have made such wildlife like this?[16]
The Father, Son, and Holy Ghost with canticum caritatis.

IV
In His Image

All living things were good having been inspected,

The Potters' love and skill[17] requires awe to be respected,[18]

The power and the glory cannot be easily rejected[19]

For Creation's crowning form has it faithfully reflected.[20]

And so up from the ashes formed from the dusty clay

Man was fashioned kindly sometime late on the sixth day.

With the breath of life within him, he was told that he should stay

In the garden with his charge of one tree to keep away.[21]

And dominion rested with Adam over all the birds and beasts,
It was his job to rule over all from the great down to the least,
Given every seed-bearing plant to provide for his feasts,[22]
Wisdom discerned graciously that loneliness increased…

Having given names to cattle, birds, and even all the sheep,
None were fit companions so They struck him fast asleep.
And to complement this Adam while he dreamt so very deep,
Eve his wife was made to have, to hold, and lovingly to keep.[23]

And when complete with a smile and nod
They said, "This is good because I AM God."
And who could have imagined an image quite like this?
The Father, Son, and Holy Ghost with canticum caritatis.

V
Love for the Fallen

Life began so peacefully in this garden paradise,
Evil was unheard of without whisper or thought of vice.
Beneath the verdant canopy placed by the gracious Lord of Life
Our first parents walked hand in hand before they were enticed.

Soon innocence betrayed them to the scheming snake,
Falling victim to temptation of forbidden fruit did take
And expected treasured knowledge whose benefits were fake,
Hid their shame with cloths of leaves that they had to quickly make.[24]

And as the Lord approached in the breezes of the wind,
And pondered disobedience, did question why they sinned,
With panic they did point the blame, but as excuses thinned,
Realized the guilt within them as Satan surely grinned.[25]

In justice LORD God judged the worm to on its belly crawl,
Then did banish man from Eden, disappointed by the fall,
But guided them with a reprimand to always heed Their call,
And as a loving Father did not abandon them at all.[26]

And when complete with a smile and nod,
They said, "This is *still* good because I AM God."
And who could have demonstrated mercy quite like this?[27]
The Father, Son, and Holy Ghost with canticum caritatis.

VI
A Planning Father

Before the foundations of the world were laid

The Master foresaw this corruption displayed

Anticipated the nature of the game to be played

And fashioned salvation to yet be perfectly portrayed.[28]

Setting strife between the devil and the offspring of the womb,

They prophesied the victory for men to avoid their doom,[29]

That in the fullness of time, the Son would dispel the gloom,[30]

By sacrificing His own life to rise and conquer the tomb.[31]

And so began the toil of the first generations of man

While the Godhead rested patiently and waited to enact the plan.[32]

Though wickedness did spread and raised Destruction's hand,

Noah's line found favor since he was a righteous man.[33]

So to purge the surface there to give the world a fresher path,

Flood waters from the primal source were sent to quench the wrath

With a worldwide deluge of a cleansing healing bath

A covenant was established with life on Earth that would always last.[34]

And when complete with a smile and nod

They said, "This is *still* good because I AM God."

And who could have started man's redemption quite like this?[35]

The Father, Son, and Holy Ghost with canticum caritatis.

VII
A Chosen People

After the destruction, Noah's line did populate[36]

And like before, the sin of men began to propagate

Filled the world with kin that wanted to be great,[37]

And in their pride, a tower built, did bring about God's fate.

Mankind was divided with linguistic aggravation,[38]

Love abided carefully and selected for salvation

A man called Abram to be the father of a nation,

Whose descendants would reveal God's Shield from condemnation.[39]

A sacred pledge inaugurated by the Holy One
Came to those, whose faith allowed the Will to be done.[40]
For the plan was set in motion for the coming of the Son,
In whose perfect righteousness, evil's work would be undone.[41]

Sincere trust placed in a call to leave his kin's abode,
Obediently departed upon an unknown road,
Followed the Lord's command of his son's life owed,
The angel stayed his hand and God's blessings overflowed.[42]

And when complete with a smile and nod
They said, "This is good because I AM God."
And who could have planned a story quite like this?
The Father, Son, and Holy Ghost with canticum caritatis.

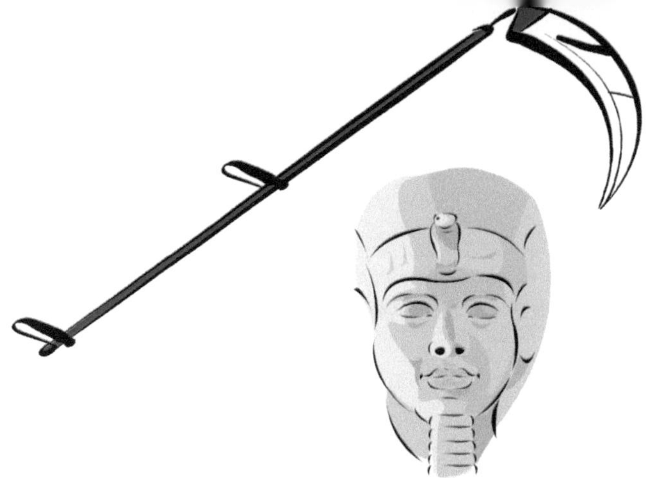

VIII
The Promise Keeper

And as the Lord decreed, this people did increase,
And though his brothers sold him, Joseph did find peace.[43]
Although the house would fall, God's foresight did not cease,
In spite of Pharaoh's slavery, They kept planning as They pleased. [44]

Blessing and cursing those who blessed and cursed the Chosen,[45]
Hearing the cry of the poor in spirit, a saving wind soon blows in,[46]
Because in spite of Pharaoh's heart utterly being frozen,
The Shepherd of Israel through epic plagues certainly did show him.

They sent Their servant Moses to warn Pharaoh as Their guide,
That They would do what They said when Their people cried.
Blood, pests, and misery did not sway the Pharaoh's pride,
And he did not relent until the worst, when every first-born died.[47]

And Passover would then mark this merciful deliverance,
A memorial time to remind them of their circumstance:[48]
That despite their feelings, they were not governed by mere chance,
The destiny of this people was in God's loving providence.[49]

And when complete with a smile and nod
They said, "This is good because I AM God."
And who could have rescued Their people with powers such as this?[50]
The Father, Son, and Holy Ghost with canticum caritatis.

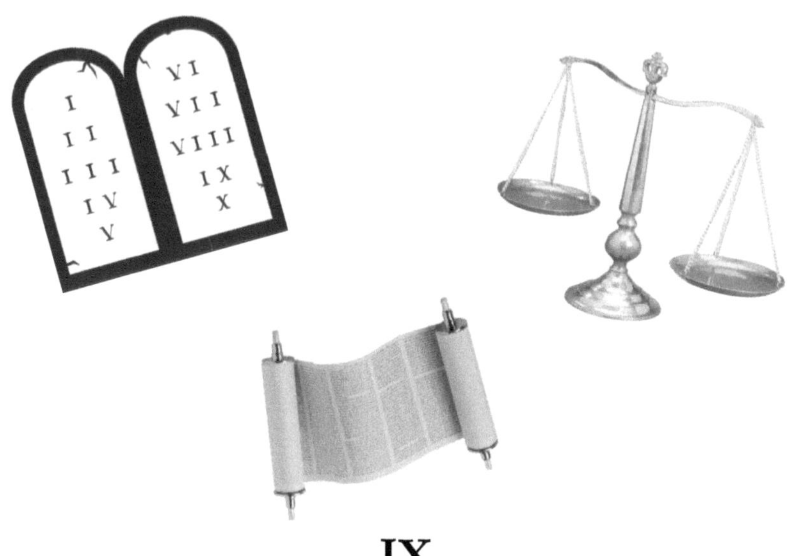

IX
The Word is Law

Escaping Pharaoh's rage across the dry Red Sea they darted,[51]

A more intimate bond with their God would soon be started,[52]

For by this connection, the fate of faithful would be guarded,

Because this Law would separate the wicked from wholehearted.[53]

It was there upon the mountain on holy ground did stand,

Moses in humility was given the Law by the Great I AM,[54]

And as a prophet, Moses did lead the fickle band

Across the barren desert toward the Promised Land.[55]

From that point on, Judgment has been clear and plain as day;[56]
Wisdom would always dictate to do what They would say:
Never trust in idols and repent when gone astray,[57]
Since the wicked would ignore and the righteous would obey.[58]

And so the kingdom Israel when following the rules
Enjoyed their God's protection from all their enemies' tools,
And despite all the miracles the people became fools,
Worshiping false idols made of gold and precious jewels.[59]

And when complete with a smile and nod
They said, "This is *still* good because I AM God."
And who could have remained with deserters quite like this?[60]
The Father, Son, and Holy Ghost with canticum caritatis.

X
Sovereign Lineage

And Israel did prosper with great judges who helped out,[61]
But even in prosperity, man's insecurity did cause doubt,[62]
And they pleaded for dear Samuel to tell their Lord about,
Their desire for a king to rule who'd be prudent, just, and stout.[63]

Compliantly God anointed Saul as Israel's first king,[64]
Until the blessed David killed Goliath with his sling,[65]
And reigned throughout a golden age, did mostly pleasing things,[66]
He praised his Lord most every day writing psalms that all would sing.[67]

And Solomon would prove to be a great leader too,[68]

When from God he asked for wisdom, his renown and fortune grew,[69]

And so a line of sovereignty was made to give another clue,

That the Son of God would come to usher the eternal reign anew.[70]

For though the Lord was the One True King, always in control,

The people had lost sight again of their obedient role,[71]

But in omniscient strategy this would just achieve the goal,

Of bringing forth a royal shoot to save the people's souls.[72]

And when complete with a smile and nod

They said, "This is good because I AM God."

And who could have nurtured a family tree like this?

The Father, Son, and Holy Ghost with canticum caritatis.

XI
Wisdom for the Ages

The history of this time recorded the pattern of man's ways,
Where fortune seemed to come to all regardless of their days.
Vanity of vanities, under the sun where cruel fate plays[73]
Though fools would surely boast, the wisest always prays,[74]

For the patience of Their Wisdom would reveal to those that trust,[75]
The Love They had for all, both the wicked and the just,
That this impartial kindness at the core was a crucial must,[76]
For They realized most graciously that every man was dust.[77]

And treating them like children, the Father taught them what was right,[78]

As Wisdom called for discipline, leading them with light,[79]

Proverbs of the shrewdest truth filled with great insight,

Granted understanding that put ignorance to flight.[80]

So setting down the precepts for happiness to thrive:

To find this wisdom and understand is a blessing when alive,[81]

Abandon all your doubts and for her knowledge always strive,

For in God's ways alone would man continue to survive.[82]

And when complete with a smile and nod

They said, "This is all good because I AM God."

And who could have taught with persistence quite like this?[83]

The Father, Son, and Holy Ghost with canticum caritatis.

XII
Hope for the Faithful

Decades became centuries and evil would often lure,

But the fear of the Lord began the paths of those who would endure,[84]

And honoring the sacrifices of all whose hearts were pure,[85]

Ritual atonement blood had become the sinners' cure.[86]

Imperfection in these practices would cause them to fall short,[87]

But of the contract that was made, God of course could not abort, [88]

And so for hope to remain, Lord sent servants to report

Of the coming of the Judge of Highest Heaven's Court.[89]

Prophets spoke on Their behalf preaching counsel and of Messiah,[90]
The Prince of Peace, the Holy Priest, of whom there is no higher,
The King of Kings, whose righteous reign would not ever expire,[91]
The Son of God would surely come and not make Them the liar. [92]

To be praised by the lowly and despised by those in power, [93]
Immanuel would soon appear in the holy appointed hour.[94]
The merits of His sacrifice would cause Satan to cower,
And the glory of the triumph would cause the Father's grace to shower.[95]

And when complete with a smile and nod
They said, "This is good because I AM God."
And who could have prophesied a message quite like this?
The Father, Son, and Holy Ghost with canticum caritatis.

XIII
The Greatest Gift

How do we express our feelings to those whom we adore?
Being in Their image, a gift can't simply come from stores,
For any such material would be better if there was more,
And so the greatest gifts are always given from our cores.

And the only thing that we can give that is truly of any worth
Is our total time, our very selves wherever there is dearth. [96]
And so it went, the Trinity chose to send the Son to Earth[97]
To save the world, the Begotten One did have a humble birth.[98]

It must not have been easy to leave behind the bliss,
Angelic choirs singing praise would certainly be missed,[99]
Along with perpetual light for the darkness of all this,
But such is Love and sacrifice to win a beloved's kiss.[100]

So willfully the Son accepted the mission of reclamation
For those with any faith were given the greatest indication,
That God so loved the world to save us from damnation,
Sent His only Son to us to secure our restoration.[101]

And when complete with a smile and nod
They said, "This is good because I AM God."
And who could have given a gift quite like this?
The Father, Son, and Holy Ghost with canticum caritatis.

XIV
Extraordinary Humility

And so it was in Galilee an angel did appear,
Announced to Virgin Mary that God's Son she would soon bear,
And though betrothed to Joseph and expecting many jeers,
With faith and full of grace, she accepted without fear. [102]

For the census they did travel to the town of David's name, [103]
The star of His arrival beckoned magi to the same, [104]
And angels called the shepherds to witness that He came, [105]
The most innocent of babies was there to take our blame.[106]

All pieces of the puzzle fit perfectly in place,
And soon it would be time for evil to be faced,
So Jesus grew in wisdom and carried it with grace,[107]
While John the Baptist cried that repentance be embraced.[108]

And if clothed in flesh had not been sufficiently so meek,
Behold! The Lamb of God was then baptized in the creek
To fulfill all righteousness and prepare to help the weak,
The Spirit as a dove descended, drove Him to the desert peaks.[109]

And when complete with assurance from above
They said, "This is the Son I AM pleased to love."[110]
And who could have raised a Savior quite like this?
The Father and The Holy Ghost with canticum caritatis.

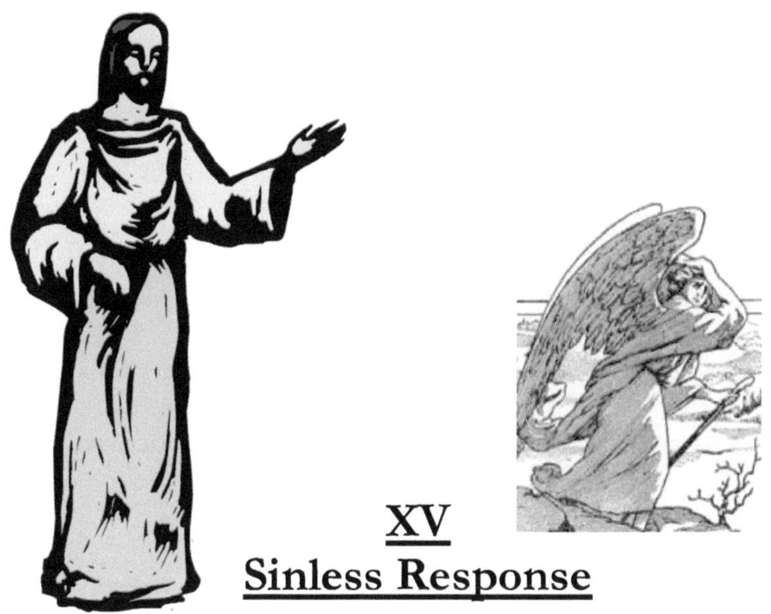

XV
Sinless Response

In the barren wasteland where He fasted and prepared,
The devil quoted scripture spinning lies as if he cared.
When told to turn the stones to bread, Jesus only glared,
And stated only on the Word is man's hunger ever spared. [111]

Again the snake did reference some lines with spiteful will,
Tempting Him to test the Lord by jumping off the hill,
For angels would surely rescue and not allow Him to be killed,
Yet Jesus shot him down again knowing of the plan to be fulfilled. [112]

And when mortal necessity and doubt did not prevail,
The devil offered wealth and power and thought he couldn't fail,
For if only he could make Him bow, he'd be the hero of his tale,
But Satan did learn slowly that his tricks would not avail.

Again, firm in His conviction, Christ did offer praise,
For the Lord alone above should we worship all our days,[113]
And accustomed to our trials, Jesus conquered Satan's ways,[114]
By keeping on the mission an unwavering fixed gaze.

And when complete with assurance from above
They said, "This is the Son I AM pleased to love."
And who could have trained a disciple quite like this?
The Father and the Holy Ghost with canticum caritatis.

XVI
The Perfect Example

This Jesus of Nazareth would wander hill and plain,

Showing mercy to the outcasts, embracing sick and lame,

Those cursed with poverty and women full of shame,

He spoke to all with kindness and never pointed blame.[115]

He ate and dined with sinners while Pharisees did mock[116]

Trying with words to trap Him, He became the stumbling block,[117]

Let him without a sin be the first to cast a rock,[118]

His boldness of both word and deed made many people talk.

Clearly this was special, a divinely sanctioned tour,
His compassion for the small made Him loved among the poor,
Sermons on morality were spoken by the shore,[119]
And His lessons were remarkable, but there was so much more.

Forgiveness instead of vengeance was quite the major theme, [120]
Before judging those for splinters, we must first remove the beam, [121]
And see our foes as neighbors and not exactly what they seem, [122]
But to love without condition; for by that code He did redeem.[123]

And when complete with assurance from above
They said, "This is the Son I AM pleased to love."
And who could have lived a selfless life like this? [124]
The Father, Son, and Holy Ghost with canticum caritatis.

XVII
Authority Incarnate

With masterful authority and with power in His speech[125]

It was the suffering oppressed that Jesus would often reach. [126]

He showed them many mysteries using parables to teach,[127]

And called on those who heard Him to practice what He preached.[128]

Though appearing in the flesh, underneath His glory shone,

The demons that had known Him as the One upon the Throne,

Recognized the Son of God and fearfully would moan,

But Jesus quickly silenced them and changed their wicked tone.[129]

For with supremacy of will having all in His control,

He drove out unclean spirits from every tortured soul,

Commanded them to hold their tongues until He achieved the goal,

The Messianic Secret was kept so that faith would take its toll.[130]

And to that end He demonstrated His true nature with a sign

Of miracles and wonders to prove He was Divine.

Cured the sick, restored blind sight, turned water into wine,

Calmed the storms, raised the dead, and made all the people fine![131]

And when complete with assurance from above

They said, "This is the Son I AM pleased to love."

And who could have displayed a power quite like this?

The Father, Son, and Holy Ghost with canticum caritatis.

XVIII
Mysterious Ways

His closest friends were thrilled their savior came at last,[132]
They did not expect however what would quickly come to pass,[133]
When all their hopes and dreams would be shattered very fast,
Even though He told them His lot had already been cast.[134]

After entering the city triumphant and full of zeal,[135]
Jesus dined with His apostles at His last Passover meal.
Judas left to go make good on his part of the wretched deal,
And away into the garden the Man to God did make appeal.

Sweating blood and fearful, Jesus intensely wept and prayed,
But in spite of this brief weakness in His humanity displayed,
He submitted and surrendered for the end game to be played,
He stood up with faith and purpose and was arrested unafraid.[136]

Mysterious it must have seemed when He was taken bound in chains.
Friends abandoned swiftly and avoiding their own pains,[137]
Unaware He went to His death to remove all of sin's stains,
To open Heaven's Gate to where God's Love forever reigns. [138]

And when complete with assurance from above
They said, "This is the Son I AM pleased to love."
And who could have sat and watched a travesty like this? [139]
The Father and the Holy Ghost with canticum caritatis.

XIX
The Consuming Passion

To an unfair trial and with false statements accused,

He spoke only truth yet they beat Him and they bruised,

Then the more He kept quiet, the more they abused,

And all the while, Satan laughed so readily amused.[140]

Though guiltless and righteous, no wrong to be found,

Pilate handed Him over to be beaten and bound,

And though His blood splattered all over the ground,

The crowd's loud call for death was the only vocal sound.[141]

So, scourged and spat on, Jesus brought the cross up to the hill,
Where ultimately His blood poured out the Father's loving will
And as He prayed for His killers, the final drop did spill,
With the victory achieved, the devil's panicked heart did chill.

For in dying blameless there, God's wrath upon Him hurting,
And a spear wound to the side confirmed with water spurting,
Jesus reconciled man to God by the tear of the Holy Curtain,
And by the grace of Love, sin's defeat would now be certain.[142]

And when complete with assurance from above
They said, "This is the Son I AM pleased to love."
And who could have let the Son die quite like this?
A perfect loving Trinity with canticum caritatis.

XX
Mysterious Ways Revealed

Upon seeing their great leader crucified right next to thieves, [143]
Hope was lost as it seemed because who could have believed
The real Messiah would let this happen and in death just simply leave?
And so fearful for their own lives, they hid where they could grieve.[144]

With the people of the covenant being like a stubborn daughter,
To reunite with the wayward flock, He passionately sought her,[145]
The Suffering Lord's Servant was led like a lamb to slaughter,[146]
Freely laid down His life and with His blood He bought her.[147]

For behind the scenes beneath the ground in the land of all the dead,
Hades could not hold back Christ, for by the blood He shed,
God would raise Him from the grave to be the Church's head,[148]
Giving life to those who loved Him because He did all that was said.

And fulfilling all the promises that the prophets had foretold, [149]
The good news of the Lord would reach the young and very old:[150]
Jesus Christ was crucified to ransom what man sold,
And in His resurrection did bring the lost back to the fold.[151]

And when complete with a smile and a nod
They said, "This is good because I AM God."
And who could have finished a masterpiece like this?
The Father, Son, and Holy Ghost with canticum caritatis.

XXI
A Holy Mission

The overjoyed apostles had seen their Lord alive,

Not a ghost, but in the flesh His life force had revived, [152]

And according to the master plan of old They had contrived

The faithful had to wait until the Advocate arrived.[153]

Christ Ascended, returned to the Father's right hand side, [154]

And sent the Holy Spirit to continue to teach and guide, [155]

So that every tongue and nation could live although they died, [156]

For evangelization every gift from then on was grace supplied.[157]

As Peter with the twelve preached the Gospel to the Jews,
They were ridiculed by some, who thought them drunk on booze, [158]
But filled with the Holy Spirit, they knew they couldn't lose,
And so boldly spread the Word of God and let every person choose.[159]

They baptized in Their Name, as was commissioned by the Son,
Prayed that all the faithful would live lovingly as one, [160]
And until earthly death had claimed them their work was never done,
For every person that they reached was another soul He won.[161]

And as the Church was born with a smile and nod,
They said, "This is good because I AM God."
And who could have left behind a legacy like this?
The Father, Son, and Holy Ghost with canticum caritatis.

XXII
Ubiquitous Spirit

The exploits of new Christians caught the focus of this man Saul,
A Pharisee of Pharisees, he persecuted Christ with gall, [162]
But in a blinding light, the Lord called out a new name: Paul, [163]
And told him plainly that His Gospel was for him to spread to all.[164]

Given mercy and forgiveness and by the Spirit riled,
With passion unparalleled and rarely ever mild, [165]
The apostle to the Gentiles preached to every man and child
How by the love and grace of God mankind was reconciled![166]

The universal savior, this Christ by dying showed,

God was the only fit one to bear sin's crushing load,

Since by the Law man always left something to be owed,

But by their faith in Christ the Lord, they walk the narrow road. [167]

This righteousness made known by God's overwhelming grace,

Apart from the law, the faith in Christ that had been placed,[168]

Would purify their hearts and let them see God's Holy Face,[169]

And allow them to finish life's challenging long race.[170]

And when complete with a smile and nod

Let them hear, "Welcome home, child, for I AM God." [171]

And who could have completed a plan as great as this?

The Father, Son, and Holy Ghost with canticum caritatis.

XXIII
Patiently Waiting

The fate of all believers by the Spirit has been sealed, [172]

The Lord of Life has come, so what more must be revealed? [173]

They wait for sinners patiently to confess and then to yield,[174]

To allow Them to dwell within and let their hearts be healed.[175]

And though defeated in the end, the devil does still labor

Taunting, causing suffering so the faithful might yet waver, [176]

So put on spiritual armored gear and use the Word your saber,

For we war against not only flesh but an essence that is graver.[177]

As time runs out for wickedness and confusion spreads like fire,

Pray and do not fear, for God calls and then inspires, [178]

All to seek a closer bond before the offer here expires,

And so the faithful witness all their days and cannot yet retire. [179]

As they linger in this life looking forward to forever,[180]

Saints by faith for certain know there's nothing here to sever

The Love of God through Christ our Lord, who won in His endeavor

Foiled all of evil's snares no matter how cruel or clever.[181]

And when complete with a smile and nod

They said, "This is good because I AM God."

And who could be so kind to those who still deny all this?

The Father, Son, and Holy Ghost with canticum caritatis.

XXIV
Final Revelation

The mysteries of Their ways require faith to fully show, [182]

But sooner or later each mortal being comes to know,

This life of theirs is brief at best and when it's time to go,

Will Death appear to the dying as a friend or evil foe? [183]

How can all this "Love" be true when such evil here succeeds?

Wars ensue, the innocent suffer, and the poor lack many needs,

When logic and reason cannot explain away such evil deeds.

How can those with hardened hearts dare to trust Their creeds?[184]

I simply cannot fathom as a lowly mortal man,
Why anyone still suffers with a Loving God at hand,
But if none have ever guessed it, what makes me think I can?
And so humbly I must trust Them, after all it is Their plan.[185]

With all avenues exhausted and submission is complete,
Accepting all fate thankfully and rejoicing in defeat,[186]
Remember even Death itself, will be crushed beneath His feet.[187]
Behold He makes all things new from His Everlasting Seat![188]

And when all has been completed with a smile and nod
They will say, "This was good because I AM God."
And who could have revealed a Love as grand as this?
The Father, Son, and Holy Ghost with canticum caritatis.

XXV
Biblical Notes & Glossary

I. The Beginning 9

1. Genesis 1:1-2; Nehemiah 9:6; Hebrews 1:10, 11:3

2. Genesis 1:3-5; Psalms 33:6-7, 9; Psalms 136:5-9

3. Job 38:7; Psalms 19:1-7; Psalms 96:11; Psalms 148:2-6; Isaiah 40:26; Romans 1:20

4. Genesis 1:6-10

5. Genesis 1:31

6. Exodus 3:11-15

II. Garden Growth..11

7. John 1:1-4

8. Genesis 1:11-13, 29-30; Psalms 96:12; Psalms 148:9; Wisdom 13:5

9. Genesis 1:14-19

10. Genesis 8:22; Revelation 21:1, 22-24

11. Genesis 2:8-9

Numbers 9:2-5; 28:16-25; Deuteronomy 16:1-8; Hebrews 11:28

49. Judith 8:15-17; Job 42:2; Psalms 33:11-12; Psalms 138:8; Isaiah 46:9-10; 55:9-11; Jeremiah 29:11; Romans 8:28; Ephesians 1:3-12

50. Deuteronomy 11:3; 26:8; Nehemiah 9:10; Judith 5:12; Psalms 4:4; Psalms 78:42-54; Psalms 105:5; Psalms 106:7-8; Wisdom 19:7-8; Jeremiah 32:20-21; Baruch 2:11

IX. The Word is Law..25

51. Exodus 14:16; Joshua 2:10; 4:23; Judith 5:13; 1Maccabees 4:9; Psalms 106:9; Psalms 136:13-15; Wisdom 10:18-19; Hebrews 11:29

52. Exodus 19:5-6; Leviticus 26:12; Deuteronomy 7:6; 14:2; 26:18-19; Ezekiel 11:19-20; Hebrews 8:10; 1Peter 2:9

53. 1Samuel 2:9; 2Samuel 22:26-27; Psalms 18:21-28; Psalms 37:28-29; Psalms 97:10; Wisdom 3:9-10

54. Exodus 20:1-22; Deuteronomy 5:6-21

55. Numbers 1-36

56. Leviticus 18:5; Deuteronomy 4:7-8, 23-31; 5:6-10, 32-33; 11:26-28; 30:15-20; Jeremiah 21:8-9; Ezekiel 20:11

57. Deuteronomy 6:12-19; 2 Chronicles 7:14-16; Jeremiah 10:14-15, 25:5; Psalms 34:15; Proverbs 3:7; 1 Peter 3:10-12

58. 1 Samuel 15:22; Proverbs 21:3; Hosea 6:1-6; Micah 6:6-8

59. Exodus 32:1-35; 1 Kings 12:28; 2 Kings 17:13-17; Jeremiah 2:5

60. Numbers 23:19; 1 Samuel 12:22; 1 Chronicles 16:14-15;

Isaiah 48:9; Jeremiah 14:21; 2 Timothy 2:13

X. Sovereign Lineage..27

61. Judges 1-21; 1 Samuel 12:9-11; Acts 13:20; Hebrews 11:32-33

62. Proverbs 15:16; Ecclesiastes 2:18-26

63. 1 Samuel 8:1-22

64. 1 Samuel 10:1,24; 11:15; Acts 13:21

65. 1 Samuel 17:4-51; 1 Maccabees 4:30;

Sirach 47:4

66. 2 Samuel 5-24; 1 Kings 1-2:11; 1 Chronicles 11-29

67. 2 Samuel 22:1-51; Psalms 18:1-51, 34:2-4, 145:1-21

68. 1 Kings 2:12-11:43; 2 Chronicles 1-9

69. 1 Kings 10:23-24; 2 Chronicles 9:22-23

70. 2 Samuel 7:12-16; 1 Kings 9:5; 1 Chronicles 22:10;

Psalms 45:7-8, 89:36-37; Daniel 2:44, 4:31, 7:13-18; Micah 4:7;

Matthew 28:18 Luke 1:30-33; Hebrews 1:8-9;

Revelation 11:15-18

71. 1 Samuel 8:7; 1 Chronicles 16:31;

Psalms 10:16-18, 93:1, 96:10, 99:1

72. Isaiah 11:1, 53:2; Jeremiah 23:5, 33:14-16; Zechariah 3:8;

Matthew 1:6-16; Luke 3:31-32; Acts 13:16-22; Revelation 22:16

XI. Wisdom for the Ages....................................29

73. Ecclesiastes 1-12

74. Proverbs 14:3,18:7; Ecclesiastes 10:12; Sirach 20:7;

1 Thessalonians 5:17

75. Psalms 18:20-28; 125:4; Proverbs 3:34; James 4:6;

1 Peter 5:5

76. Exodus 34:6; Leviticus 19:18; Psalms 86:15, 103:8, 145:7-8; Sirach 2:11, 4:9-10; Isaiah 1:17; Jeremiah 31:3; Zechariah 7:9-10; Matthew 5:43-48; Luke 6:27, 32-36; Romans 13:9; Galatians 5:14; James 2:8

77. Genesis 2:7, 3:19, 18:27; Job 10:9, 34:15; Psalms 90:3, 103:14; Ecclesiastes 3:20, 12:7; Sirach 10:9

78. Hosea 2:1; Romans 9:26

79. Deuteronomy 8:5; Judith 8:27; Psalms 94:12, 119:105; Proverbs 6:23; Hebrews 12:5-11; Revelation 3:19

80. Proverbs 3:1-26

81. Proverbs 3:13-15, 8:21, 34-35; Wisdom 7:8-11; Sirach 1:13-21

82. Psalms 62:1-13, 118:8, 146:3; Proverbs 4:1-27

83. Psalms 100:5, 118:1, 136:1-26; Isaiah 40:28

XII. Hope for the Faithful....................................31

84. Psalms 111:10; Proverbs 1:7, 9:10; Job 28:28; Sirach 1:16

85. 1 Samuel 15:22; Psalms 51:18-19; Proverbs 21:3; Matthew 9:13, 12:7

86. Exodus 30:10; Leviticus 17:11; Romans 3:24-26

87. Hosea 6:6; Amos 5:22-24; Micah 6:6-8

88. Isaiah 49:15-16; Jeremiah 32:40; Ezekiel 16:59-63

89. Psalms 67:5, 96:13, 98:8-9; Ecclesiastes 3:17, 11:9; Isaiah 2:1-5, 11:4; Micah 4:1-4; James 4:12

90. Deuteronomy 18:15-22; Jeremiah 33:14-16; Malachi 3:1; John 6:14; Acts 3:22, 7:37 (Isaiah, Jeremiah, Baruch, Ezekiel, Daniel, Hosea, Joel, Amos, Obadiah, Jonah, Micah, Nahum, Habakkuk, Zephaniah, Haggai, Zechariah, Malachi)

91. Isaiah 9:5-6; Luke 1:32-33; 1 Timothy 6:15-16;

Revelation 19:16

92. Psalms 12:7, 19:8; Habakkuk 2:3; Romans 5:5-6; Galatians 4:4-7

93. Isaiah 53:1-12

94. Isaiah 7:14; Matthew 1:23

95. Romans 3:21-26; 5:1-21, 8:28-39; Ephesians 1:7, 2:8; Titus 3:7-8

XIII. The Greatest Gift..33

96. Romans 12:6-8; 1 Corinthians 10:31; 2 Corinthians 9:6-7; Colossians 3:23; 1 Peter 4:8-11

97. John 3:16-18; 1 John 4:9

98. Matthew 1:18-23, 2:1-15; Luke 2:6-14

99. Job 38:4-7; Psalms 103:20, 148:2; Daniel 3:58, 7:9-10: Revelation 4:8, 5:11

100. John 1:1-5, 14; 1 Corinthians 8:6; Philippians 2:5-8; Colossians 1:16

101. Isaiah 53:9-12; Matthew 1:21; John 3:16-18; Romans 4:13-25

XIV. Extraordinary Humility...............................35

102. Luke 1:26-56

103. Micah 5:1; Luke 2:1-7

104. Psalms 72:10-15; Isaiah 60:6; Matthew 2:1-12

105. Luke 2:8-14

106. 1 John 2:2, 4:10

107. Luke 2:39-40, 51-52

108. Isaiah 40:3; Matthew 3:1-3; Mark 1:1-8; Luke 3:1-18; John 1:6-28; Acts 13:22-25, 19:4

109. Matthew 3:13-17, 4:1; Mark 1:9-12; Luke 3:21-22, 4:1;

John 1:29-34

110. Matthew 3:16-17, 17:1-8; Mark 1:9-11, 9:2-8;

Luke 3:21-22, 9:28-36

XV. Sinless Response……………………………………37

111. Deuteronomy 8:3; Matthew 4:1-4; Mark 1:12-13;

Luke 4:1-4

112. Exodus 17:1-7; Deuteronomy 6:16; Psalms 91:11-12;

Matthew 4:5-7; Luke 4:9-12

113. Deuteronomy 6:13, 10:20; Matthew 4:8-10; Luke 4:5-8

114. Isaiah 53:3; Hebrews 2:17-18, 4:14-16, 5:1-3

XVI The Perfect Example………………………..39

115. Isaiah 57:18-19; Matthew 4:23-25, 9:35; Mark 1:14-45;

Luke 4:14-15, 42-44, 5:15, 8:1; Ephesians 2:17-18

116. Matthew 9:9-13; Mark 2:13-17; Luke 5:27-32, 15:1-2, 19:7

117. Psalms 118:22-23; Isaiah 8:12-15, 28:16; Matthew 21:42-45;

Luke 2:34; Acts 4:5-12; Romans 9:30-33; 1 Corinthians 1:18-25;

1 Peter 2:4-12

118. Deuteronomy 17:7; John 8:1-11

119. Matthew 5-7, 12:33-35; Luke 6:20-49

120. Sirach 28:1-5; Matthew 6:12-15; 18:21-22, 35; Mark 11:25;

Luke 11:4, 17:3-4; James 2:13

121. Wisdom 12:22; Matthew 7:1-5, 23:24-28; Mark 4:24;

Luke 6:37-42, 11:39-41; Romans 2:1-2; 1 Corinthians 4:5

122. Matthew 5:43-45, 7:12; Luke 6:31, 10:29-37

123. Leviticus 19:18; Proverbs 10:12, 17:9; Hosea 1:7;

Zechariah 4:6; Matthew 5:43-48, 19:19, 22:37-39;

137. Zechariah 13:7; Matthew 26:31, 56; Mark 14:27, 50-52; John 16:32

138. John 1:29; Hebrews 9:1-28; Revelation 7:13-17

139. Isaiah 53:10

XIX. The Consuming Passion.....................45

140. Wisdom 2:19; Isaiah 50:6, 53:7; Matthew 26:57-68; Mark 14:53-65; Luke 22:63-71; John 18:19-24; Acts 8:30-35;

141. Matthew 27:11-26; Mark 15:1-15; Luke 23:1-25; John 18:28-40, 19:1-16

142. Matthew 27:27-56; Mark 15:16-39; Luke 23:26-47; John 19:17-37

XX. Mysterious Ways Revealed...........................47

143. Isaiah 53:12; Mark 15:27; Luke 23:32-33, 39-43

144. Mark 16:14; John 20:19-20

145. Ezekiel 34:11-16; Matthew 15:24; Luke 15:4-10, 19:10

146. Isaiah 53:7

147. Acts 20:28; 1 Corinthians 6:19-20, 7:23; Ephesians 1:7; Colossians 1:20

148. 1 Corinthians 11:3; Ephesians 4:15, 5:23; Colossians 1:18

149. Psalm 22:1-32; Isaiah 53:1-12; Daniel 9:24; Luke 24:25-27, 44; Acts 3:11-26; 1 Peter 1:10-11;

150. Daniel 7:14; Matthew 28:18-20; Mark 16:14-15; Luke 2:10, 24:44-47; Acts 1:8

151. 2 Corinthians 5:18-19; Colossians 1:20; Romans 5:1-11

XXI. A Holy Mission..49

152. Matthew 28:1-20; Mark 16:1-11; Luke24:1-48; John 20:1-31, 21:1-25

153. Luke 24:49; John 14:15-18, 26; Acts 1:4-8

154. Psalms 110:1; Mark 16:19-20; Luke 24:50-53; Acts 1:9-11; Hebrews 1:1-4, 8:1; Ephesians 1:20; 1 Peter 3:22

155. Psalms 104:30; Acts 2:1-4, 15:8

156. John 5:24, 8:51, 11:25-26

157. Romans 12:1-8; 1 Corinthians 12:1-11; 2 Corinthians 4:7; Ephesians 4:7-16; 1 Peter 4:10-11

158. Acts 2:1-13; 1 Corinthians 14:1-25

159. Acts 9:27-28, 14:3, 18:24-28, 19:8; Ephesians 6:19-20; Philippians 1:12-14; 2 Timothy 2:9

160. Acts 4:32-35; Romans 15:5; 1 Corinthians 1:10; Ephesians 4:1-6; Philippians 2:1-3; Colossians 3:14-15; 1 Peter 3:8

161. 1 Corinthians 9:19-27, 10:33; 2 Corinthians 4:7-18; 1 Timothy 4:16; James 5:19-20; Jude 1:21-23

XXII Ubiquitous Spirit......................................51

162. Acts 7:58, 8:1-3, 9:1-2

163. Acts 9:3-30; 22:1-21; 26:1-23;

164. Psalms 119:46; Romans 1:5-16, 10:9-17; 1 Corinthians 1:18-25; Ephesians 3:1-13

165. Acts 9:28; 18:1-28; 19:8-12; Romans 12:11; 1 Corinthians 16:22; 2 Corinthians 13:2; Galatians 1:6-10; Philippians 1:20-26; 3:7-11

166. John 3:16-17; Acts 13:16-39; Romans 5:1-11; 6:23; 2 Corinthians 5:18-21; Galatians 2:15-21; Ephesians 1:3-10; 2:8-9; Colossians 1:13-22; 1 Timothy 1:12-17; 2:1-7; Titus 3:3-7; 1 John 1:2; 4:14

167. Matthew 7:13-14; Romans 13:14; Galatians 5: 1-25;

1 Thessalonians 5:21-22; 2 Timothy 2:14-26; Hebrews 12:1-2; James 1:1-27; 1 Peter 2:1-3, 16

168. Acts 10:34-43; Romans 3:21-26; Galatians 2:16; 3:11; Ephesians 2:8-9; Philippians 3:1-11;

169. Psalms 24:4-5; 73:1; Matthew 5:8

170. Romans 5:3-5; 1 Corinthians 9:24-27; Philippians 3:12-15; 1 Timothy 6:12; 2 Timothy 2:1-7; 4:6-8; Hebrews 12:1-2; James 1 :1-27; Revelation 2:10

171. Matthew 25:20-23; Luke 19:16-19; 2 Peter 1:3-11

172. Romans 8:14-17; 2 Corinthians 1:21-22; Ephesians 1:13-14; 4:30

173. Romans 16:25-27; Ephesians 1:7-10; 3:4-5; Colossians 1:24-28; 1 Peter 1:20-21

174. Ezekiel 18:23; 1 Timothy 2:3-6; 2 Peter 3:1-10

175. Jeremiah 31:33; Ezekiel 11:19-20; 36:26; John 14:23; 1 Corinthians 3:16; 2 Corinthians 3:3; Hebrews 10:16; Revelation 3:20

176. John 10:10; 1 Peter 5:8-11;

177. Romans 13:12; 2 Corinthians 6:3-10; 10:3-5; Ephesians 6:10-17

178. Isaiah 55:6-7; Romans 13:11-14; 1 Corinthians 10:13; 2 Corinthians 5:14-15; 12:9-10; James 4:6-9

179. Acts 20:24; 2 Corinthians 4:3-6; 2 Timothy 4:1-8; 1 Peter 3:13-17

180. 2 Corinthians 5:1-10; Philippians 1:20-26

181. Wisdom 3:1; Isaiah 43:13; John 6:37-40; 10:28-29;

Romans 8:38-39

182. 1 Corinthians 1:21 ; Corinthians 5:7; Hebrews 11:3,6

183. Proverbs 27:1; Psalms 39:5-6; 62:10; 90:9-10; 144:4; Job 14:1; Ecclesiastes 6:12; James 4:13-17

184. Deuteronomy 30:15-20; Matthew 5:3; 24:4-14; 1 Corinthians 1:18-25; 2:14; Galatians 6:7-10; 2 Thessalonians 2:1-12; 1 Timothy 4:1; 2 Timothy 4:3-4; James 4:1-12; 2 Peter 3:3; 1 John 3:4-5; Jude 1:18

185. Job 11:7-8; Psalms 131:1; 139:6; Wisdom 9:13; Sirach 3:21-23; Isaiah 40:12-31, 55:8-11; Jeremiah 23:8; Romans 11:30-36; 1 Corinthians 2:1-16

186. 1 Corinthians 10:31; 1 Thessalonians 5:16-18; Ephesians 5:20; Philippians 4:4-9; Colossians 3:17

187. Psalms 110:1; Isaiah 25:8; John 12:31-32; Romans 6:9; 1 Corinthians 15:20-28, 53-55; 2 Timothy 1:9-10; Hebrews 2:14; 10:12-13; Revelation 1:18; 20:11-15; 21:4

188. Isaiah 43:18-19; Revelation 21:5

Glossary – All words appear in the order in which they appear within each chapter. All definitions and synonyms are derived from entries retrieved from http://www.merriam-webster.com/ copyright 2015 by Merriam-Webster, INC.

I. The Beginning

1. Eternal – having no beginning or end in time, lasting forever.
2. Abyss – a hole or space that is immeasurably deep.
3. Ceaseless – continuous or constant.
4. Loam – a type of soil that is good for growing plants.
5. Cosmos – the universe, especially when it is understood as an ordered system.
6. Canticum Caritatis – A Latin phrase referring to a song or poem about love and charity.

II. Garden Growth

1. Godhead – the divine essence; especially refers to the Holy Trinity when capitalized.
2. Abound – to be present in large numbers or in great quantity.
3. Plea – a serious and emotional request for something.
4. Prolifically – producing fruit freely in great amounts.

III. The Living Planet

1. Leviathan – an extremely large sea monster
2. Teemed – became filled or overflowed.
3. Comply – to do what you have been asked.

IV. In His Image

1. Fashioned – formed something into or from something else.
2. Charge – the responsibility given from an instruction.

3. Dominion – the power to rule.
4. Discerned – to come to know or recognize.
5. Complement – something that completes or makes perfect.

V. Love for the Fallen

1. Paradise – a very beautiful, peaceful place of happiness
2. Vice – a moral flaw, weakness, or bad habit.
3. Verdant – green with a variety of growing plants.
4. Enticed – attracted or tempted by arousing hope and desire.
5. Pondered – to think about or consider something carefully.
6. Banish – to force, drive out, or expel
7. Reprimand – a severe or formal scolding, reproof, or rebuke.
8. Heed – pay attention to warnings or advice.

VI. A Planning Father

1. Corruption – state of impurity, defiled virtue or moral principle.
2. Portrayed – shown in a certain way.
3. Enact – to perform or officially establish something into law.
4. Purge – to clear something of guilt or free it from moral corruption.
5. Primal – very basic, powerful, and original.
6. Quench – to put to a satisfying end.
7. Wrath – divine retribution, intense/harsh but just punishment for wrongdoing.
8. Deluge – a flooding overflow of water.
9. Covenant – a formal, serious, and sacred agreement or promise.
10. Redemption – the act of making something better… in Christianity, saving people from sin, evil and death.

VII. A Chosen People

1. Propagate – to cause to spread out and affect a greater number or greater area.
2. Linguistic – related to language.
3. Condemnation – an official statement or expression of very strong and definite criticism and blame.
4. Inaugurated – officially introduced.
5. Abode – the place where someone lives.

VIII. The Promise Keeper

1. Decreed – to command through an order usually having the force of law or religious authority.
2. Foresight – the ability to see what will or might happen in the future.
3. Utterly – completely, totally, absolutely
4. Mere – used to describe or indicate that something is small or unimportant.
5. Providence – divine guidance or care.

IX. The Word is Law

1. Intimate – having a very close, friendly and loving relationship.
2. Fickle – changing ways and opinions often, marked by a lack of constancy or stability.
3. Repent – to feel and show genuine remorse/sorrow for what you have done wrong and the desire to do what is right.

X. Sovereign Lineage

1. Sovereign – a king or queen, one who exercises supreme authority.

2. Prosper/prosperity – to become very successful; the state of being successful.
3. Prudent – having or showing careful good judgment.
4. Compliantly – ready and willing to comply accordingly to a set of standards.
5. Renown – great fame and respect.
6. Omniscient – knowing everything, having unlimited knowledge or understanding.
7. shoot – a new branch or part of a plant, including that of a "family tree."

XI. Wisdom for the Ages

1. Vanity – something that is vain, empty, or valueless.
2. Impartial – not partial or biased, treating or affecting everyone equally.
3. Shrewdest – mentally sharp or clever.
4. Precepts – a rule that says how people should behave; a command or principle intended as a general rule of conduct.

XII. Hope for the Faithful

1. Atonement – reparation for an offense or injury; the reunion of God and humankind through the sacrificial death of Jesus Christ.
2. Messiah – the expected anointed king and deliverer of the Jews.
3. Merits – the spiritual credit held to be earned by performance of righteous acts and ensure future benefits.

XIII. The Greatest Gift

1. Dearth – the state or condition of not having enough of something.

2. Begotten – past tense of beget: to produce as an effect or cause to exist.* In reference to the relational nature of the Trinity: "They are distinct from one another in their relations of origin: '...It is the Father who generates, the Son who is begotten, and the Holy Spirit who proceeds." (CCC 254)
3. Perpetual – continuing forever.
4. Reclamation – restoration, recovery
5. Damnation – the state of being in hell as punishment after death.

XIV. Extraordinary Humility

1. Betrothed – promised to be married.
2. Beckoned – to signal someone to come closer or to follow.
3. Magi – members of a priestly class among the ancient Medes and Persians. Used to identify the three wise men/kings paying homage to the infant Jesus.
4. Meek – having or showing a quiet and gentle nature.

XV. Sinless Response

1. Spiteful – having or showing a desire to harm, anger, or defeat someone.
2. Prevail – to defeat an opponent especially in a long or difficult contest.
3. Avail – be of use or serve as an advantage.
4. Conviction – a strong belief or opinion.

XVI. The Perfect Example

1. Pharisees – 'separated.' - a member of a Jewish sect of the intertestamental period noted for strict observance of rites and ceremonies of the written law and for insistence on the validity of their own oral traditions concerning the law.

2. Sanctioned – given effective or authoritative approval or consent.
3. Vengeance – retaliation for having been hurt by another; revenge.

XVII. Authority Incarnate

1. Incarnate – having a human body.
2. Parables – short stories that teach moral or spiritual lesson; a common instructional tool of Jesus to teach about the Kingdom.

XVIII. Mysterious Ways

1. Lot – one's way of life or worldly fate.
2. Triumphant – rejoicing for or celebrating victory or success.
3. Zeal – a strong enthusiastic feeling that makes someone eager or determined to do something.
4. Wretched – very bad or unpleasant.
5. Travesty – something shocking, upsetting, or ridiculous because it is not what it is supposed to be or what is expected. A grossly inferior imitation.

XIX. The Consuming Passion

1. Passion – the sufferings of Jesus between the night of the Last Supper and his crucifixion; an intense, driving, compelling feeling or conviction.
2. Scourged – struck or hit with a whip as means of punishment.
3. Reconciled – to have caused 2 groups separated by arguments/disagreements to become friendly again.

XX. Mysterious Ways Revealed

1. Sought – past tense of seek… to have searched out.
2. Hades – the underworld, the home of the dead in Greek mythology; ruler of the underworld.
3. Ransom – to free from captivity or punishment by paying a price.

XXI. A Holy Mission

1. Advocate – someone who argues or works for a cause, policy, group or person. When capitalized, in Christianity, the term refers to the Holy Spirit.
2. Ascended – to rise up toward the sky/heaven.
3. Evangelization – preaching the Gospel message.
4. Commissioned – to order or request to make or do something.
5. Legacy – something transmitted by or received from an ancestor, predecessor, or the past.

XXII. Ubiquitous Spirit

1. Ubiquitous – existing or being everywhere at the same time; widespread.
2. Exploits – exciting acts or actions, notable deeds.
3. Gall – blatant boldness coupled with disrespectful assurance.
4. Unparalleled – having no equal; never seen or experienced before.

XXIII. Patiently Waiting

1. Saber – a long, heavy sword with a curved blade.
2. Graver – more likely to produce great harm or danger; more serious.
3. Endeavor – serious determined effort and activity directed toward a goal.
4. Foiled – prevented from achieving an end; brought to nothing.

XXIV. Final Revelation

1. Ensue – to happen as a result.
2. Creeds – ideas and beliefs that guide the actions of people.

www.ingramcontent.com/pod-product-compliance
Ingram Content Group UK Ltd.
Pitfield, Milton Keynes, MK11 3LW, UK
UKHW041920190726
13854UKWH00003B/1354